CONCISE JUNIOR DICTIONARY EXERCISES

Edited by **Iseabail Macleod**
and **Patrick McLaughlin**
with **Alasdair Anderson**

Schofield & Sims Ltd. Huddersfield

0 7217 0647 9

First Printed 1989
Reprinted 1991

Designed by Graphic Art Concepts, Leeds
Illustrated by Barry and Tim Davies
Printed in England by Smiths Colour Printers

Foreword

This book consists of a series of dictionary exercises based on *A Concise Junior Dictionary*. The exercises are planned on the assumption that the child has never before used a dictionary nor had any experience of alphabetical arrangement.

A brief summary of the approach is as follows:

Unit 1

Exercises 1–5   Alphabetical arrangement based on the letters at the beginning of words.

Exercise 6   Use of the dictionary.

Completion of sentences based on:

Unit 2   The Natural World

Unit 3   People and Things

Unit 4   Fantasy and Imagination

A child who has worked systematically through the exercises should then be able to use a dictionary, or any similar reference book, with little or no guidance.

The questions have been devised, not only to give practice in the use of a dictionary, but also to expand the general knowledge of the children. For this reason, the exercises are grouped under topics.

Answers are included at the back of the book to allow children to mark their own or other children's work, should the teacher so desire.

UNIT 1 · How to use the Dictionary

Here is the Alphabet

A B C D E F G H I J K L M N O P Q R S T U V W X Y Z

a b c d e f g h i j k l m n o p q r s t u v w x y z

This is how words are put into a dictionary.

First come all the words beginning with **a**. Then words beginning with **b**. This goes on through the alphabet till you reach the words beginning with **z**.

This is called **alphabetical order**. It is used in a large number of books where lists of words or names are used. The names in the telephone directory, for example, are in alphabetical order.

We will begin with some exercises to let you become used to working with alphabetical order.

Exercise 1

1 What is the first word in this dictionary?

2 What is the last word in this dictionary?

3 What is the first of the **r** words?

4 What is the last of the **g** words?

5 What is the first of the **t** words?

6 What is the last of the **b** words?

7 What is the first of the **m** words?

8 What is the last of the **o** words?

9 What is the last of the **c** words?

10 What is the first of the **q** words?

11 What is the last of the **a** words?

12 What is the first of the **h** words?

13 What is the last of the **t** words?

14 What is the first of the **z** words?

15 What is the last of the **d** words?

Check with the answers at the back of the book.

Exercise 2

A	B	C	D	E	F	G	H	I	J	K	L	M	N	O	P	Q	R	S	T	U	V	W	X	Y	Z
a	b	c	d	e	f	g	h	i	j	k	l	m	n	o	p	q	r	s	t	u	v	w	x	y	z

Here are some groups of words. Put each group into the correct alphabetical order.
Keep checking with the alphabet at the top of the page till you know it by heart.

1 zebra   ape   lion

2 gooseberry   plum   coconut
strawberry

3 maple   beech   oak   holly
sycamore

6 tulip   crocus   dandelion
primrose   lily   hyacinth
buttercup

7 treacle   marzipan   syrup
liquorice   custard   dessert

8 locust   finch   kangaroo
gazelle   dragonfly   ostrich
jackal

4 donkey   gull   lobster
alligator   shark   horse

5 radish   celery   turnip
onion   parsnip

Check with the answers at the back of
the book.

Exercise 3

But what do you do when a number of words start with **the same letter**?

For example: <u>chimpanzee</u>   <u>crocus</u>   <u>cactus</u>.

You look at the **second** letter and put the words into the alphabetical order of the second letter.

Since in the alphabet **a** comes before **h**, and **r** comes after **h**, the correct alphabetical order of the above words is:

<u>cactus</u>   <u>chimpanzee</u>   <u>crocus</u>.

Quite simple, really, isn't it?

Here are some groups of words with the same first letter. See if you can put them into their correct alphabetical order.

1 <u>h</u>olly   <u>h</u>erb   <u>h</u>azel

2 <u>p</u>ineapple   <u>p</u>eanut   <u>p</u>lum
<u>p</u>alm

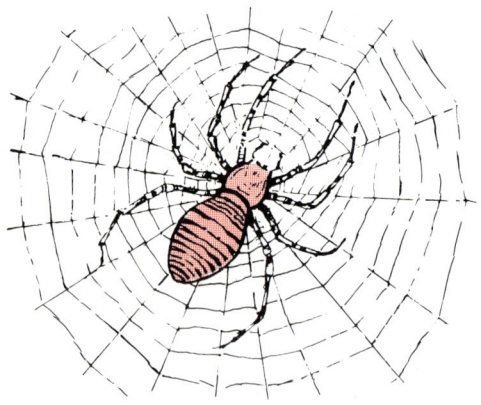

3 <u>s</u>pider   <u>s</u>kylark   <u>s</u>heep
<u>s</u>tallion   <u>s</u>erpent

4 <u>c</u>amel   <u>c</u>uckoo   <u>c</u>haffinch
<u>c</u>rab

5 <u>m</u>ysterious   <u>m</u>onster
<u>m</u>arvellous   <u>m</u>ischievous

6 <u>w</u>indmill   <u>w</u>histle   <u>w</u>riggle
<u>w</u>easle

7 <u>p</u>ython   <u>p</u>anther   <u>p</u>enguin
<u>p</u>orpoise   <u>p</u>igeon   <u>p</u>heasant

8 <u>a</u>quarium   <u>a</u>ntelope   <u>a</u>crobat
<u>a</u>valanche   <u>a</u>lphabet

Check with the answers at the back of the book.

Exercise 4

What do you think happens when the first **two** letters of a word are the same?

For example: **banjo**　　　**bazaar**　　　**badger**.

Well, you look at the **third** letter and put the words into their alphabetical order using this letter.

In the alphabet **n** comes before **z** and after **d**, so the correct dictionary order of the above words is:

　　　badger　　　**banjo**　　　**bazaar**.

Here are some groups of words with the same **first** and **second** letter. Put them into their correct alphabetical order.

1　**magpie**　　**mammal**　　**mackerel**

2　**poodle**　　**porpoise**　　**poppy**

3　**lark**　　**ladybird**　　**lamb**

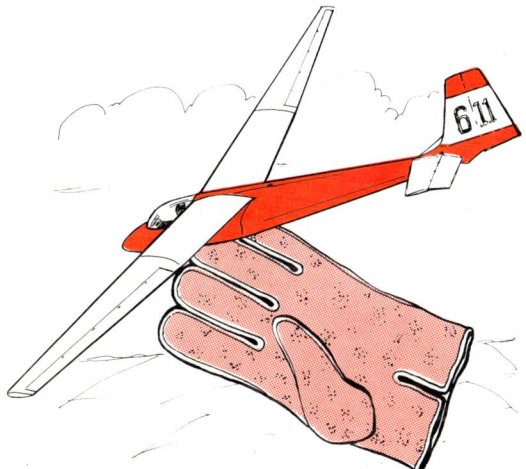

4　**glider**　　**glove**　　**glue**　　**glass**

5　**quiz**　　**question**　　**quarter**　　**quote**

6　**unwell**　　**unhappy**　　**universe**　　**understand**　　**uncommon**

7　**juggler**　　**judo**　　**junior**　　**juice**

8　**thunder**　　**thrilling**　　**thermometer**　　**thistle**

Check with the answers at the back of the book.

Exercise 5 *(Revision)*

Put the following words into their correct alphabetical order. Watch out for words which begin with the **same letter** or **letters**.

1   **kidney   magnificent
splinter   marble**

2   **palace   shipwreck   paddle
quiver**

3   **turban   tweed   raspberry
primrose**

4   **unicorn   munch   wobble
mussel**

5   **camouflage   kipper   cackle
kilt**

6   **apple   anorak   oyster
ostrich**

7   **gnaw   hamster   gnome
halter   hatchet**

8   **hockey   humble   hoarse
honour   huge**

Check with the answers at the back of the book.

Exercise 6 — Words at the top of the page

There is one other thing you need to know about how dictionaries are set out on the page. Look at page 6 in your Concise Junior Dictionary.

Here is the top of the page from the dictionary:

actress			agree
actress	a woman who performs in a play, a film or on television.	**advance**	to move forward.
		adventure	an exciting happening.
actual	real; existing.	**advertise**	to make well-known (for example in a newspaper)

Can you work out for yourself why the two words are put at the top of the page above the black line?

That's right. The one on the left is the first word on the page and the one on the right is the last word on the page.

As usual the words in between are all in **alphabetical order**.

These words are there to save you time and trouble.

If the word you are looking for is between these two words, then this is the page you look at closely.

If the word isn't between these two words, then you don't have to waste your time going through every word. You move on quickly.

It is good to get into the habit of glancing at these words at the top first when you are looking for a word in a dictionary, or a name in a telephone directory. This habit will save you hours of time in the end.

Here is an exercise to help you get used to using them.

Draw this table in your exercise book. The entry for **blazer** is given as an example. In your own table write down the words listed below and fill in the rest of the information about each one.

	Word	Page number	Word at top left	Word at top right
1	blazer	14	better	bleat
2	parachute			
3	camera			
4	hammock			
5	trumpet			
6	ginger			
7	wicket			
8	gallon			
9	kiss			
10	instrument			

UNIT 2 · The Natural World

In the exercises that follow look up each word in **heavy type** in your dictionary. Then write down and complete the sentences which are started for you.

Exercise 1   *Places – wet and dry*

1 A **ravine** is ....

2 A **bog** is ....

3 A **stream** is ....

4 A **forest** is ....

5 A **loch** is ....

6 A **river** is ....

7 A **mountain** is ....

8 A **desert** is ....

9 An **ocean** is ....

10 A **valley** is ....

11 An **oasis** is ....

12 An **iceberg** is ....

13 A **jungle** is ....

14 A **sea** is ....

15 A **coast** is ....

16 A **moor** is ....

17 A **waterfall** is ....

18 A **lake** is ....

19 An **island** is ....

20 A **cliff** is ....

Exercise 2 — Sky and weather

1. **Drizzle** is . . . .

2. **Weather** tells you . . . .

3. A **cloud** is . . . .

4. **Dusk** is . . . .

5. When it is **chilly**, you feel . . . .

6. **Slush** is . . . .

7. A **rainbow** is . . . .

8. **Climate** is the . . . .

9. The **horizon** is the . . . .

10. **Lightning** is . . . .

Exercise 3 — Natural disasters

1. A **volcano** is a . . . .

2. **Famine** means that people are . . . .

3. A **blizzard** is . . . .

4. A **typhoon** is . . . .

5. An **avalanche** is . . . .

6. A **hurricane** is . . . .

7. **Plague** is . . . .

8. **Drought** is when for a long time . . . .

9. An **earthquake** is . . . .

10. A **flood** is . . . .

11

Exercise 4 — Trees

1 What grows on a **bramble** bush?

2 What does a **maple** tree produce?

3 Where does **moss** grow?

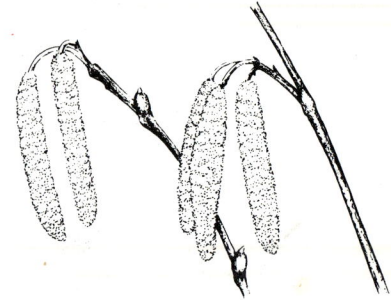

6 What word would you use to describe the flowers of the **catkin**?

7 What kind of stems does **bamboo** have?

8 What colour is the bark of the **beech** tree?

9 What kind of trees would you expect to find in an **orchard**?

4 What do we use **hedges** for?

5 What is another name for **maize**?

10 Where does **heather** grow?

Exercise 5 — Flowers

1 What colour is a **buttercup**?

2 What kind of shape does the flower of a **tulip** have?

4 Where would you find a **cactus** growing?

5 In what season of the year do **hyacinths** grow?

3 What colour are the petals of a **daisy**?

Exercise 6   Vegetables

1 What colour is the flesh of a **turnip**?

2 What does a **leek** taste a bit like?

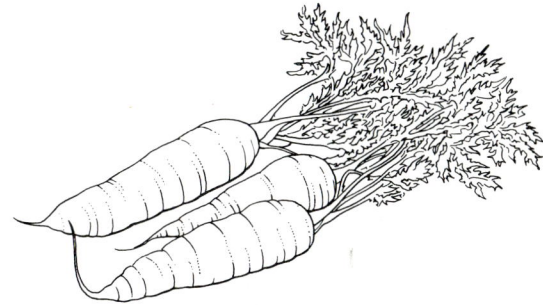

3 What colour is the flower of the **cauliflower**?

4 What kind of vegetable is a **carrot**?

5 What kind of stalks does **rhubarb** have?

Exercise 7   Fruit

1 What colour is a **lemon**?

2 What do you find inside a **peach**?

3 What is a **fig** full of?

4 What is a **damson**?

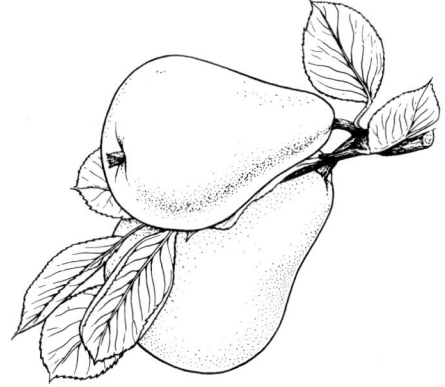

5 What kind of shape does a **pear** have?

6 Where do **pineapples** grow?

7 What colour are **grapes** usually?

8 What is a **grapefruit** like?

9 What is a **tangerine** like?

10 Where do **strawberries** grow?

Exercise 8 — Creatures which live in water

1 What is unusual about a **dolphin**?

2 What do these fish have in common: **cod**, **mackerel**, **haddock**?

3 Why do people gather **oysters** from the sea-bed?

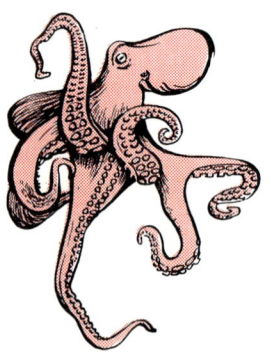

4 How many arms has an **octopus**?

5 Why would you keep well away from a **shark**?

6 Which sea-animal is a **porpoise** like?

7 What does a **lobster** have to protect itself?

8 What kind of water does a **trout** live in?

1 What is the usual colour of a **ladybird**?

2 Why does a **spider** make a web?

3 What does a **dragonfly** look like?

4 What kind of skin does a **lizard** have?

5 What is the first thing you notice about a **butterfly**?

6 How does a **python** kill its victims?

7 What does a **beetle** do with its wings when it isn't flying?

8 What is another name for a **serpent**?

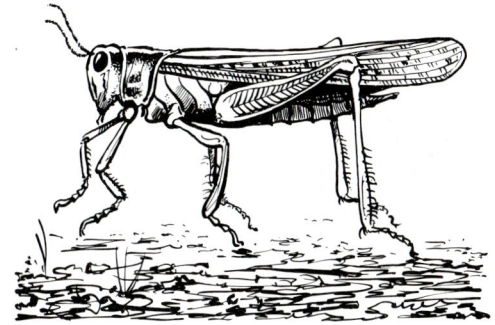

9 What is a **grasshopper** especially good at?

10 Why do African farmers fear **locusts**?

11 What do **gnats** do that is unpleasant?

12 What does a **wasp** look like?

Exercise 10   *Facts about animals*

Look up the words in **heavy type** in your dictionary. In your exercise book answer these questions. Your answers should be in sentences.

1 What do **hyenas** eat?

2 What does a **gazelle** look like?

3 What colour is a **panda**?

4 What do all **monkeys** have?

5 What colour is a **panther**?

7 What kind of fur does a **leopard** have?

8 What kind of skin does a **toad** have?

9 What does a **hedgehog** have on its back?

6 Where do **kangaroos** come from?

10 What would you use a **ferret** for?

11 In which part of the world would you find **reindeer**?

12 Where would you most likely find a **hippopotamus**?

13 What kind of tail does a **squirrel** have?

14 How does a **frog** move about?

15 What does an **otter** eat?

16 In which part of the world would you find **beavers**?

17 What does a **rhinoceros** have on its nose?

18 What does a **jackal** look like?

19 What colour is a **badger**'s face?

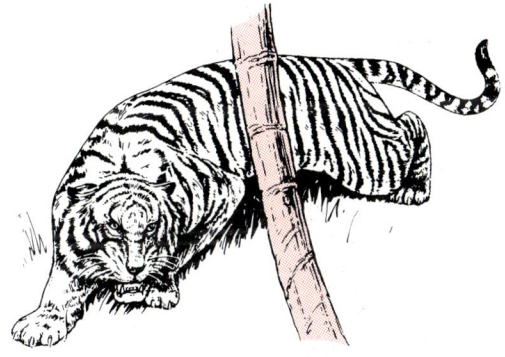

20 What colour are a **tiger**'s stripes?

21 What does a monkey have that a **chimpanzee** doesn't have?

Use your dictionary to answer the following questions. Write the answers in your exercise book. Remember to write **in sentences**.

1 What colour is a **crow**?

2 What does a **vulture** eat?

6 When would you be likely to hear an **owl**?

7 Which bird is the larger, a **raven** or a **sparrow**?

8 What can you say about the cry of a **crow**?

3 In what way is a **penguin** like an **ostrich**?

4 Where does a **cuckoo** lay its eggs?

5 What colour is a **magpie**?

9 What is unusual about a **parrot**?

10 What kind of beak does a **stork** have?

11 Are **sparrows** found near houses?

12 Where would you be likely to see a **swan**?

13 What is unusual about a **pheasant**?

14 What does an **eagle** eat?

15 Where does a **pelican** store its food?

16 What colour is a **canary**?

17 What kind of noise does a **pigeon** make?

18 Why do small birds fear the **hawk**?

19 Where would you look if you heard a **skylark** sing?

20 Where would you expect to find a **gull**?

UNIT 3 · People and Things

Exercise 1

The pictures show a number of tools which are used about the house or garden. Here is a list of these tools, but not in the same order as the pictures.

spade	**drill**	**pliers**	**torch**	**ruler**
file	**shears**	**barrow**	**saw**	**screw**
pincers	**rake**	**fork**	**binoculars**	**nail**
trowel	**string**	**hammer**	**ladder**	**thermometer**

Write this exercise out in your Exercise Book.

First, find the word that matches each picture.

Then, after looking up the word in your dictionary, finish each sentence by writing down what each tool is and what it does.

1 Number 1 is a pair of . . . . They are used for . . . .

2 Number 2 is a . . . . It is used for . . . .

3 Number 3 is a . . . . It is used for driving in . . . .

4 Number 4 is a . . . . It is used for . . . .

5 Number 5 is a . . . . It is a . . . .

6 Number 6 is a . . . . It is used to . . . .

7 Number 7 is a . . . . It is used for . . . .

8 Number 8 is a pair of . . . . They are used for . . . .

9 Number 9 is a . . . . It is a cutting tool with . . . .

10 Number 10 is a pair of . . . . These are used to . . . .

11 Number 11 is a . . . . It is used for . . . .

12 Number 12 is a . . . . It is used for . . . .

13 Number 13 is a . . . . It is a special nail with . . . .

14 Number 14 is a . . . . It is used to . . . .

15 Number 15 is a . . . . This is a tool for . . . .

16 Number 16 is a pair of . . . . They have jaws which . . . .

17 Number 17 is a . . . . This is an . . . .

18 Number 18 is a . . . . This is used for . . . .

19 Number 19 is a ball of . . . . It is made of . . . .

20 Number 20 is a . . . . This is like . . . .

Tools

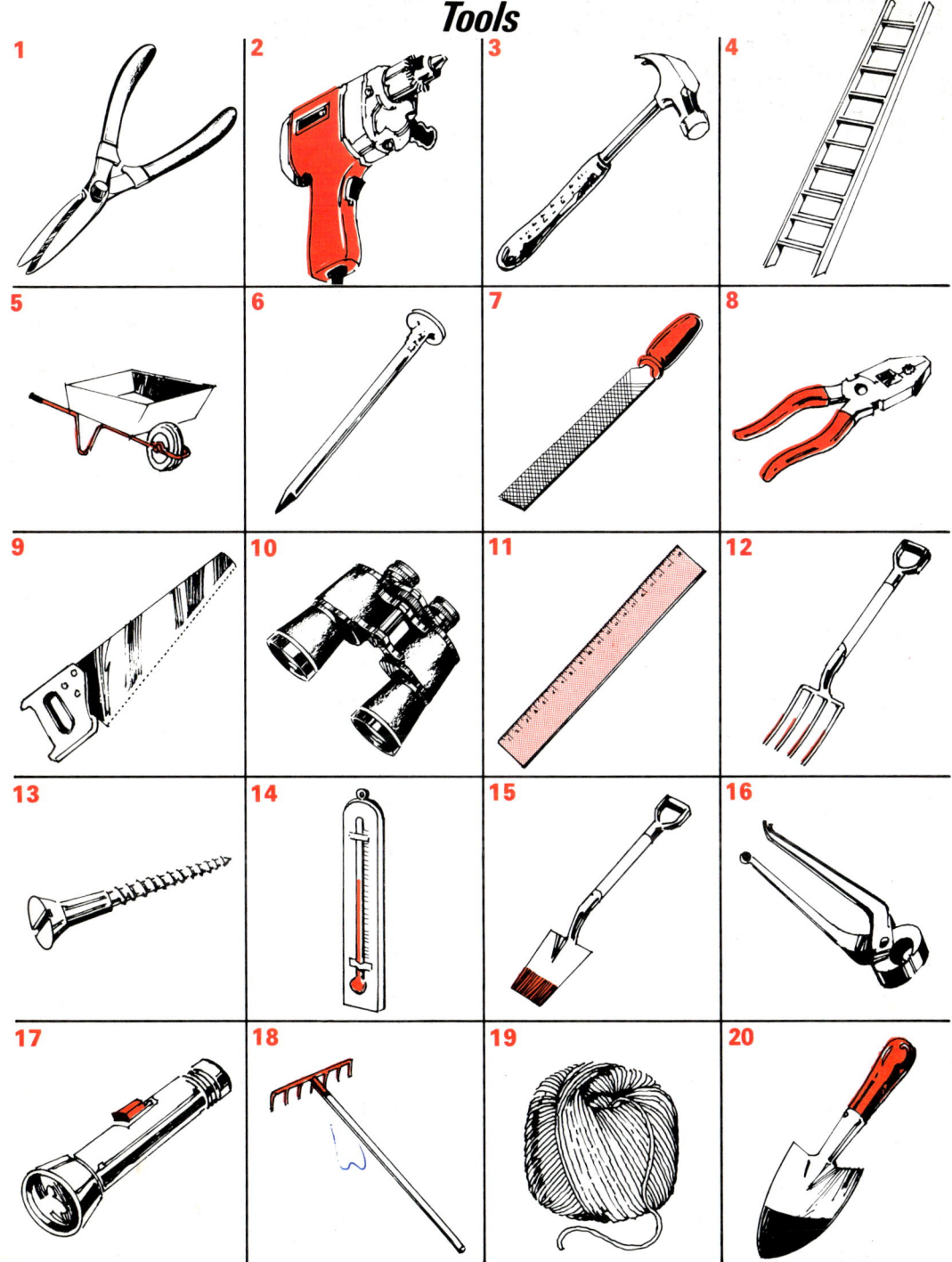

1
2
3
4
5
6
7
8
9
10
11
12
13
14
15
16
17
18
19
20

The pictures in this exercise show people at work.

In your exercise book write down what each person does.

Sometimes you can tell this from the special clothes they wear when they are working.

To help you, the first **two** letters of each word are given.

Look up each word in the dictionary to make sure you spell it correctly.

1 Number 1 is a **de**_ _ _ _ _.

2 Number 2 is a **fi**_ _ _ _ _.

3 Number 3 is a **jo**_ _ _ _.

4 Number 4 is a **te**_ _ _ _ _.

5 Number 5 is a **bu**_ _ _ _ _.

6 Number 6 is a **pi**_ _ _.

7 Number 7 is a **do**_ _ _ _.

8 Number 8 is a **di**_ _ _.

9 Number 9 is a **nu**_ _ _.

10 Number 10 is a **so**_ _ _ _ _.

11 Number 11 is a **fa**_ _ _ _.

12 Number 12 is a **ha**_ _ _ _ _ _ _ _.

13 Number 13 is a **bi**_ _ _ _.

14 Number 14 is a **sa**_ _ _ _.

15 Number 15 is an **as**_ _ _ _ _ _ _.

People at work

Look up these words in your dictionary:

umpire   **surgeon**   **florist**

secretary   **optician**.

Now **in a sentence** say what it is that each one does.

Exercise 4   *Places where people live, work and play*

Look up the words in **heavy type** in your dictionary. In your exercise book finish off the sentences which are started for you.

1   A **convent** is . . . .

2   A **wigwam** is . . . .

3   A **nursery** is a room or building for . . . .

4   An **igloo** is a . . . .

5   A **monastery** is a . . . .

6   A **cemetery** is a . . . .

7   An **aquarium** is a . . . .

8   A **stadium** is a . . . .

24

Exercise 5

Look up the words in **heavy type** in your dictionary. Then, in your exercise book, write out and finish the sentences started for you.

1 A **surgery** is a place where . . . .

2 A **factory** is a place where . . . .

3 A **theatre** is a building where . . . .

4 A **museum** is a building where . . . .

5 A **restaurant** is a place where . . . .

6 A **cinema** is a place where . . . .

7 A **hospital** is a place where . . . .

Exercise 6

Look up the words in **heavy type** in your dictionary. Then, in your exercise book, write out and finish the sentences started for you.

1 A **balcony** is a . . . .

2 A **storey** is . . . .

3 The **ceiling** is the . . . .

4 A **bungalow** is a house with . . . .

5 The **basement** is . . . .

6 A **gable** is the . . . .

7 A **cellar** is a . . . .

8 A **steeple** is a . . . .

25

In these two exercises, first look up the words in **heavy type** in your dictionary. Then, in your exercise book, write down and finish off each sentence which is started for you.

Exercise 7 — *Articles of furniture*

1 A **cupboard** is a . . . .

2 A **video** is a machine . . . .

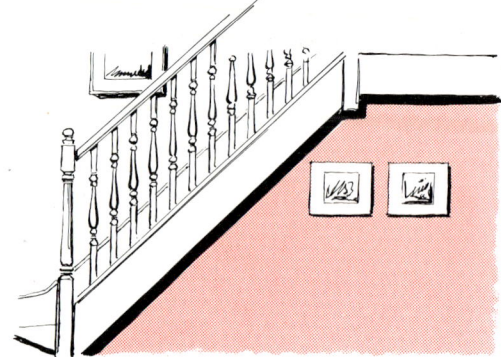

3 A **banister** is a . . . .

4 A **cradle** is a . . . .

5 A **stereo** is a . . . .

6 A **duvet** is a . . . .

7 A **mirror** is a . . . .

8 A **cushion** is a . . . .

9 A **clock** is a . . . .

10 A **couch** is a . . . .

Exercise 8 — *Things you wear*

1 A **uniform** is . . . .

2 **Jeans** are . . . .

3 A **turban** is . . . .

4 An **anorak** is . . . .

5 **Wellingtons** are . . . .

6 A **cardigan** is . . . .

7 **Pyjamas** are the . . . .

8 A **shawl** is . . . .

9 A **brooch** is . . . .

10 A **track suit** is the . . . .

Things about the house

Look up each word in **heavy type** in your dictionary.

In your exercise book finish each of the following sentences by saying what each item is or what it is used for.

1 An **oven** is used for . . . .

2 You use a **spoon** for . . . .

3 A **sink** is used for . . . .

4 A **saucepan** is . . . .

5 A **vase** is . . . .

6 You carry a **bucket** by holding the . . . .

7 A **recipe** is . . . .

8 A **broom** is . . . .

9 You find a **spout** on a . . . .

10 **Tweezers** are used for . . . .

11 A **ladle** is a . . . .

12 A **telephone** is an . . . .

13 You use a **thimble** when you are . . . .

14 **Soap** is . . . .

15 A **knife** is a . . . .

16 A **needle** is a . . . .

17 **Scales** are used in the kitchen for . . . .

18 A **kettle** is used to . . . .

19 A pair of **scissors** is a . . . .

20 You use **polish** to make things . . . .

27

Exercise 10

Look up all the words in **heavy type** in your dictionary. Then write these sentences in your exercise book filling in the blanks.

1 To **chuckle** is to laugh . . . .

2 A **clang** is the noise made by a large . . . .

3 You **gasp** usually when you are . . . .

4 A **whine** is like a . . . cry.

5 A **gurgle** is like the noise made by . . . leaving a . . . .

6 You **moan** when you are in . . . or . . . .

7 To **gobble** your food means to eat it . . . and . . . .

8 When you **whisper** you . . . very quietly.

9 You **groan** when you are . . . .

10 A **rustle** is a noise like . . . being moved.

Exercise 11 *Noises*

Below is a list of noises. Write this list in your exercise book. Opposite each word write down which animal makes a noise like this. The first is given as an example.

howl	**purr**	**squeak**	**grunt**
chirp	**quack**	**cackle**	**bleat**

Noise	*Made by*
howl	a **wolf**

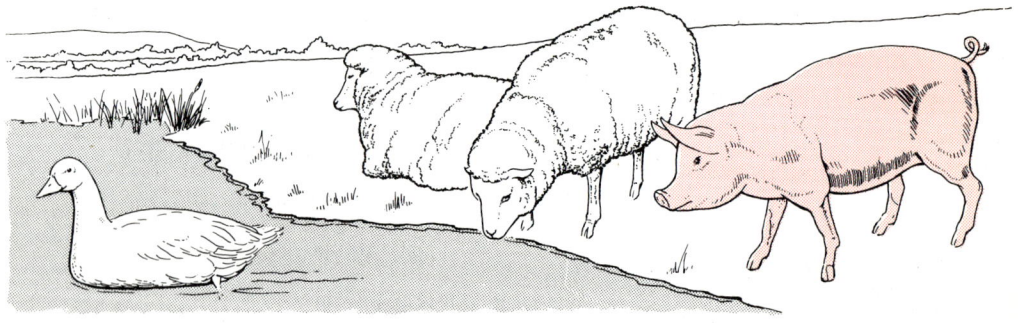

1 Where would you put **marzipan** once you've made it?

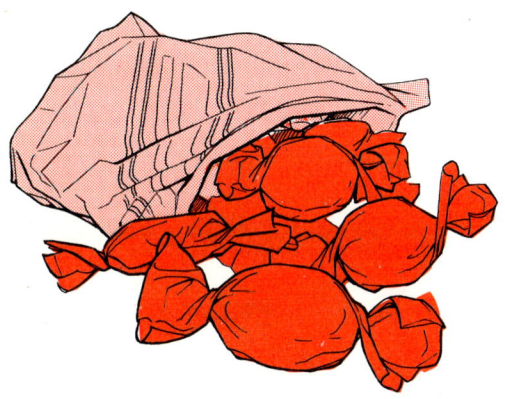

2 What kind of a sweet is a **caramel**?

3 What kind of liquid is **syrup**?

6 What fruits is **marmalade** usually made of?

7 What colour is **liquorice**?

4 What do you usually find inside a **tart**?

5 What is **peppermint** used in besides sweets?

8 What kind of cake is a **sponge**?

9 When does a **dessert** come in a meal?

10 What is **treacle** made from?

Look up the words in **heavy type** in your dictionary.
In your exercise book write out the sentences that follow, filling in the blanks.

1 A **conjuror** is another name for a . . . .

2 **Draughts** is a game played on a board with . . . .

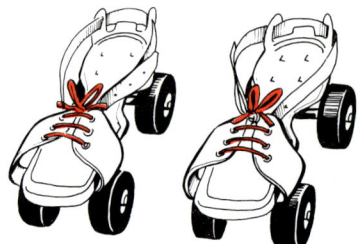

3 You make a **roller-skate** by attaching . . . to a boot or shoe.

4 **Cricket** is a game played with a . . . , . . . and . . . .

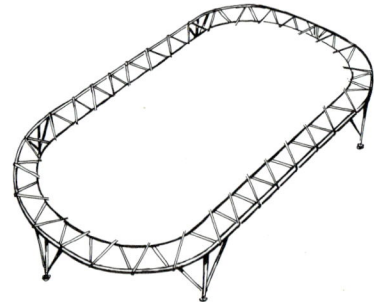

5 You can . . . up and down on a **trampoline**.

6 An **artist** is a person who makes . . . or . . . .

7 You play **billiards** on a . . . .

8 A **domino** is a piece of wood or plastic with . . . on it.

9 A **jigsaw** is a kind of . . . .

10 You use your . . . to play **volleyball**.

11 You move a **canoe** by using a . . . .

12 A **puppet** is a kind of . . . .

13 A **tricycle** has . . . wheels.

14 A **bicycle** has . . . wheels.

15 A **skateboard** is a flat . . . on . . . .

Exercise 14 — *Musical instruments*

Look up the words in **heavy type** in your dictionary.
In your exercise book write out these sentences filling in all blanks.

1 A **trumpet** is made of . . . .

2 You play a **piano** by pressing the . . . .

3 A **cello** is like a large . . . .

4 An **orchestra** is group of . . .
playing together.

5 A **guitar** has . . . strings.

6 You play a **xylophone** by hitting bars of wood or metal using a . . . .

7 You play a **clarinet** by . . . through it.

8 You hold a **violin** under your . . . .

9 An **organ** has many . . . and is played like a . . . .

10 You play a **banjo** by . . . the . . . .

31

UNIT 4 · Fantasy and Imagination

Exercise 1 — *Magic, mystery and the supernatural*

Look up the words in **heavy type** in your dictionary and then answer the questions that follow. Write these out fully in sentences in your exercise book.

A 1 A **dragon** is a . . . animal you find in stories.

2 A kind of giant that . . . is called an **ogre**.

3 A **spirit** is another word for . . . .

4 What is a **legend**?

5 An **elf** is a . . . fairy.

6 What does a **unicorn** look like?

7 A **fairy** is an imaginary person with . . . .

8 A **goblin** is a . . . fairy.

9 What kind of powers does a **wizard** have?

10 Where is a **gnome** supposed to live?

11 Where would you expect to find a **hermit**?

12 What is a **fable**?

13 A **serpent** is another and more evil-sounding name for a . . . .

14 A **dwarf** is much . . . than a normal person.

15 **Magic** is the name for those . . . and . . . things that happen by a . . . power.

B 1 Something which is **imaginary** is not . . . .

2 A **haunted** house is one which is visited by a . . . .

3 **Peculiar** is another word for . . . .

4 If something is **hideous**, it is . . . to look at.

5 If you are **invisible** you are . . . .

6 **Dreadful** means . . . .

7 If something is **curious** it means that it is . . . or . . . .

8 **Evil** means . . . .

9 When something is puzzling and . . ., we say it is **mysterious**.

10 If you say something looks **queer**, it means it is . . . or . . . .

Exercise 2

Make up a story of strange or evil doings using **at least** seven of the words in **heavy type** in Exercise 1.

Look up the words in **heavy type** in your dictionary. Rewrite or complete the sentences that follow in your exercise book. Make sure you always write a full sentence.

A 1   A **dungeon** is a . . . below ground.

2   A **knight** in olden times was a . . . .

3   What would you shoot an **arrow** from?

4   A **highwayman** made his living by stopping . . . and robbing them.

5   A **lance** is a long, thin . . . .

6   A knife with a short . . . which is . . . on both sides is called a **dagger**.

7   A **banquet** is a large . . . .

8   You keep . . . in a **quiver**.

9   A **castle** is a large building with . . . and strong . . . .

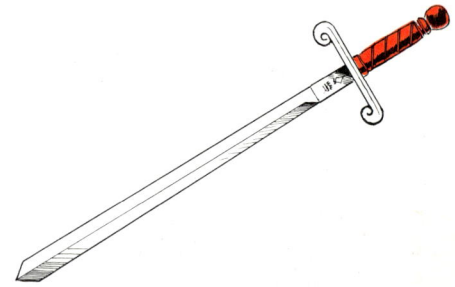

10   A **sword** is like a . . . two-sided . . . .

11   What do you buy with a **ransom**?

12   A **feast** is a large . . . meal.

13   A **tapestry** is pictures or patterns in . . . or . . . worked on heavy . . . .

14   **Armour** was the metal . . . soldiers wore in . . . in olden times.

15   A **duel** is a . . . between . . . people using the same sort of . . . .

B 1 **Marvellous** is another word for . . . .

2 A deep . . . is called **crimson**.

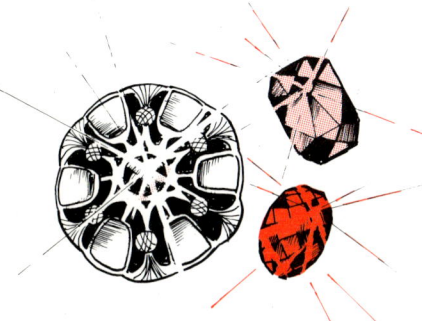

3 Something which is . . . and . . . is called **brilliant**.

4 **Magnificent** is another word for . . . .

5 To **glitter** is to . . . .

6 If you are **innocent**, then you are not . . . .

7 **Splendid** means very . . . or very . . . .

8 A **delicate** thing would be easily . . . .

9 If someone says you are **beautiful**, then you can be sure you are . . . good.

10 You **dazzle** someone by blinding them for a . . . with a . . . light.

Exercise 4

Make up a story of olden times using **at least** five of the words in **heavy type** in Exercise 3.

Answers

UNIT 1
Exercise 1

1	abandon	**9**	cylinder
2	zoo	**10**	quack
3	rabbit	**11**	axle
4	gypsy	**12**	habit
5	tabby	**13**	tyre
6	buzz	**14**	zebra
7	machine	**15**	dye
8	oyster		

Exercise 2

1 ape lion zebra
2 coconut gooseberry plum strawberry
3 beech holly maple oak sycamore
4 alligator donkey gull horse lobster shark
5 celery onion parsnip radish turnip
6 buttercup crocus dandelion hyacinth lily primrose tulip
7 custard dessert liquorice marzipan syrup treacle
8 dragonfly finch gazelle jackal kangaroo locust ostrich

Exercise 3

1 hazel herb holly
2 palm peanut pineapple plum
3 serpent sheep skylark spider stallion
4 camel chaffinch crab cuckoo
5 marvellous mischievous monster mysterious
6 weasel whistle windmill wriggle
7 panther penguin pheasant pigeon porpoise python
8 acrobat alphabet antelope aquarium avalanche

Exercise 4

1 mackerel magpie mammal
2 poodle poppy porpoise
3 ladybird lamb lark
4 glass glider glove glue
5 quarter question quiz quote
6 uncommon understand unhappy universe unwell
7 judo juggler juice junior
8 thermometer thistle thrilling thunder

Exercise 5 *(Revision)*

1 kidney magnificent marble splinter
2 paddle palace quiver shipwreck
3 primrose raspberry turban tweed
4 munch mussel unicorn wobble
5 cackle camouflage kilt kipper
6 anorak apple ostrich oyster
7 gnaw gnome halter hamster hatchet
8 hoarse hockey honour huge humble

Exercise 6 *Words at the top of the page*

	Word	Page number	Word at top left	Word at top right
1	blazer	14	better	bleat
2	parachute	86	pamper	parson
3	camera	20	cable	cape
4	hammock	56	habit	hanger
5	trumpet	134	trolley	toy
6	ginger	51	garden	giraffe
7	wicket	142	whirl	wire
8	gallon	50	funny	garbage
9	kiss	66	kettle	know
10	instrument	63	inhabit	island

UNIT 2
Exercise 1 *Places – wet and dry*

1 A **ravine** is a very deep, steep-sided, narrow valley.
2 A **bog** is wet earth, a swamp.
3 A **stream** is a small river.
4 A **forest** is a large area of woodland.
5 A **loch** is a Scottish lake.
6 A **river** is a long, wide stream of water, usually flowing into the sea.
7 A **mountain** is a very high hill.
8 A **desert** is a large, empty place where hardly anything grows because of heat and lack of water.
9 An **ocean** is a very large sea.
10 A **valley** is low ground between two hills or mountains.
11 An **oasis** is a place in the desert where water can be found and some plants grow.
12 An **iceberg** is a very large piece of ice floating in the sea.

Answers

13 A **jungle** is a thick forest in very hot countries.
14 A **sea** is the salt water which surrounds the land on the earth's surface.
15 A **coast** is the strip of land next to the sea.
16 A **moor** is a large area of rough ground, covered with grass and heather.
17 A **waterfall** is a stream or river falling from a height.
18 A **lake** is a large stretch of water with land all round it.
19 An **island** is a piece of land with water all round it.
20 A **cliff** is high, steep land often overlooking the sea.

Exercise 2   Sky and weather

1 **Drizzle** is light rain falling gently.
2 **Weather** tells you the kind of day it is.
3 A **cloud** is a mass of rainy mist floating in the sky.
4 **Dusk** is the beginning of darkness just after sunset.
5 When it is **chilly**, you feel quite cold.
6 **Slush** is half-melted, watery snow.
7 A **rainbow** is curved stripes of different colours sometimes seen in the sky in rainy weather.
8 **Climate** is the sort of weather a place usually has.
9 The **horizon** is the line where the earth and the sky seem to touch.
10 **Lightning** is a flash of light you see in the sky during a thunderstorm.

Exercise 3   Natural disasters

1 A **volcano** is a mountain which throws out melting rock, hot ashes, steam and flames.
2 **Famine** means that people are without food for a very long time.
3 A **blizzard** is a strong wind with heavy snow.
4 A **typhoon** is a great storm.
5 An **avalanche** is a large amount of snow suddenly rushing down a mountainside.
6 A **hurricane** is a storm with a very strong wind.
7 **Plague** is a terrible disease which spreads quickly.
8 **Drought** is when for a long time no rain falls and there is not enough water.
9 An **earthquake** is when part of the earth's surface shakes.
10 A **flood** is when water overflows from rivers and lakes on to roads and fields.

Exercise 4   Trees

1 blackberries
2 a syrup
3 on wet stones and trees
4 to separate fields or gardens
5 sweet corn
6 fluffy
7 stiff and hollow
8 grey
9 fruit trees
10 on moorlands

Exercise 5   Flowers

1 bright yellow
2 bell-shaped
3 white
4 in the desert
5 spring

Exercise 6   Vegetables

1 white or yellowish
2 an onion
3 white
4 a root vegetable
5 juicy

Exercise 7   Fruit

1 yellow
2 a large, hard seed called a stone
3 tiny seeds
4 a small, dark-purple plum
5 a pointed shape
6 in hot countries
7 green or purple
8 a large orange
9 a small, sweet orange
10 on very small plants

Exercise 8   Creatures which live in water

1 It is a *warm-blooded* sea animal.
2 They are all used as food.
3 To eat them.
4 eight
5 because it is dangerous and has sharp teeth
6 a dolphin
7 claws
8 fresh water

Exercise 9   Insects and reptiles

1 red with black spots
2 to catch insects for food
3 It is a long insect with fine wings.
4 skin like a snake
5 its brightly-coloured wings
6 it squeezes them to death
7 it folds them to form a hard back
8 a snake
9 jumping
10 because they destroy crops
11 they bite
12 it has black and yellow stripes

Answers

Exercise 10 *Facts about animals*

1 other animals and dead bodies
2 a small deer
3 black and white
4 a long tail and hands and feet like a person
5 black
6 Australia
7 spotted fur
8 rough skin
9 prickles
10 hunting rabbits
11 cold northern countries
12 near water in Africa
13 a bushy tail
14 by jumping
15 fish
16 in cool lands
17 one or two horns
18 a dog
19 black and white
20 black and orange
21 a tail

Exercise 11 *Facts about birds*

1 black
2 flesh
3 it cannot fly
4 in other birds' nests
5 black and white
6 at night
7 a raven
8 it is loud and rough
9 it can learn to talk
10 long and straight
11 yes
12 in the water
13 it has a long tail
14 small animals
15 in a pouch under its beak
16 yellow
17 a soft noise
18 because it hunts them for food
19 up in the sky
20 near the sea

UNIT 3
Exercise 1

1 **shears**, cutting hedges
2 **drill**, making holes
3 **hammer**, nails
4 **ladder**, getting up to high places
5 **barrow**, small cart that is pushed
6 **nail**, join pieces of wood together
7 **file**, making things smooth
8 **pliers**, gripping and cutting things
9 **saw**, sharp, pointed teeth
10 **binoculars**, let you see far into the distance
11 **ruler**, measuring or drawing straight lines
12 **fork**, digging and lifting things
13 **screw**, grooves round it
14 **thermometer**, measure heat and cold
15 **spade**, digging soil
16 **pincers**, grip when closed

17 **torch**, electric light which can be carried about
18 **rake**, scratching the earth, gathering dead leaves, etc.
19 **string**, thin cord
20 **trowel**, like a small spade

Exercise 2

1 dentist
2 fireman
3 jockey
4 teacher
5 butcher
6 pilot
7 doctor
8 diver
9 nurse
10 soldier
11 farmer
12 hairdresser
13 bishop
14 sailor
15 astronaut

Exercise 3

An **umpire** is the person who makes sure that a game is fairly played.

A **surgeon** is a doctor who carries out operations.

A **florist** is a person who sells flowers.

A **secretary** is a person whose job it is to write letters, make arrangements, etc. for another person or for an organisation.

An **optician** is a person who fits you with glasses or contact lenses to improve your eyesight.

Exercise 4
Places where people live, work and play

1 A **convent** is a building in which nuns live.
2 A **wigwam** is a North-American Indian's tent.
3 A **nursery** is a room or building for young children.
4 An **igloo** is a house made of snow blocks by eskimos.
5 A **monastery** is a place where monks live.
6 A **cemetery** is a place where people are buried.
7 An **aquarium** is a glass or plastic container in which fish are kept.
8 A **stadium** is a large open-air sports ground with rows of seats.

Exercise 5

1 A **surgery** is a place where doctors and dentists work.
2 A **factory** is a place where goods are made by machinery.
3 A **theatre** is a building where plays are acted.
4 A **museum** is a building where old and interesting things can be seen.

Answers

5 A **restaurant** is a place where you can buy food and eat it there.

6 A **cinema** is a place where films are shown.

7 A **hospital** is a place where sick people are cared for.

Exercise 6

1 A **balcony** is a raised floor in a theatre or cinema. *or* a platform outside a window.

2 A **storey** is one floor of a building.

3 The **ceiling** is the inside of the roof of a room.

4 A **bungalow** is a house with all its rooms on one floor.

5 The **basement** is a room or space under a building.

6 A **gable** is the pointed end wall of a building.

7 A **cellar** is a store-room under a building.

8 A **steeple** is a pointed tower on top of a church.

Exercise 7 *Articles of furniture*

1 A **cupboard** is a place with shelves for storing things.

2 A **video** is a machine which records and plays back films and television programmes.

3 A **banister** is a handrail beside a staircase.

4 A **cradle** is a rocking bed for a baby.

5 A **stereo** is a machine for playing tapes and records which has two speakers.

6 A **duvet** is a padded bed cover.

7 A **mirror** is a piece of glass in which you can see yourself.

8 A **cushion** is a pillow which is often used on a chair.

9 A **clock** is a machine for telling the time.

10 A **couch** is a seat for more than one person.

Exercise 8 *Things you wear*

1 A **uniform** is special clothing worn by people of the same group.

2 **Jeans** are trousers made from strong, usually blue, cotton.

3 A **turban** is a head-covering made from a long strip of material wound in a special way round the head.

4 An **anorak** is a waterproof jacket with a hood.

5 **Wellingtons** are long, rubber boots.

6 A **cardigan** is a short, woollen jacket.

7 **Pyjamas** are the trousers and jacket top worn in bed.

8 A **shawl** is a covering for the head and shoulders or for wrapping a baby.

9 A **brooch** is an ornament which can be pinned to your clothing.

10 A **track suit** is the loose trousers and top sometimes worn over sports clothes.

Exercise 9 *Things about the house*

1 An **oven** is used for cooking and baking.

2 You use a **spoon** for stirring tea, eating pudding, etc.

3 A **sink** is used for washing dishes in a kitchen.

4 A **saucepan** is a metal container with a handle used for cooking.

5 A **vase** is a container for holding flowers.

6 You carry a **bucket** by holding the handle.

7 A **recipe** is a list of instructions telling you how to cook something.

8 A **broom** is a stiff brush with a long handle.

9 You find a **spout** on a kettle or a teapot.

10 **Tweezers** are used for getting hold of things.

11 A **ladle** is a large, deep spoon with a long handle, used for serving soup, etc.

12 A **telephone** is an instrument which carries someone's voice by wire, using electricity.

13 You use a **thimble** when you are sewing.

14 **Soap** is a fatty substance used with water for washing.

15 A **knife** is a sharp blade with a handle, used for cutting.

16 A **needle** is a thin, sharp piece of metal with a hole at one end, used for sewing.

17 **Scales** are used in the kitchen for weighing things.

18 A **kettle** is used to boil water.

19 A pair of **scissors** is a cutting tool with two blades fastened together in the middle.

20 You use **polish** to make things smooth and bright by rubbing.

Exercise 10

1 quietly
2 bell
3 surprised
4 dog's
5 water leaving a container
6 in pain or unhappy
7 greedily and noisily
8 speak
9 hurt
10 paper

Answers

Exercise 11 Noises

Noise	Made by
howl	a wolf
purr	a cat
squeak	a mouse
grunt	a pig
chirp	young birds and some insects
quack	ducks
cackle	a hen
bleat	sheep and lambs

Exercise 12 Things that are good to eat

1 on cakes
2 a chewy sweet
3 thick, sticky and sweet
4 jam or fruit
5 toothpastes
6 oranges and lemons
7 black
8 a soft, light cake
9 at the end
10 sugar

Exercise 13 Sport and pastimes

1 magician
2 black and white squares
3 wheels
4 ball, bat and stumps
5 bounce
6 pictures or sculpture
7 table
8 dots
9 puzzle
10 hand
11 paddle
12 doll
13 three
14 two
15 board on wheels

Exercise 14 Musical instruments

1 brass
2 keys
3 violin
4 musicians
5 six
6 small hammer
7 blowing
8 chin
9 pipes, piano
10 plucking the strings

UNIT 4
Exercise 1
Magic, mystery and the supernatural

A
1 fire-breathing
2 eats people
3 a ghost
4 a story from long ago, which may not be true
5 small
6 a horse with one long horn
7 magic power
8 wicked
9 magic
10 under the ground
11 in a lonely place
12 a story or legend which teaches you something
13 snake
14 smaller
15 strange, wonderful, strange

B
1 real
2 ghost
3 strange, unusual
4 terrible, ugly, frightening
5 not able to be seen
6 very bad, terrible
7 strange, unusual
8 very bad, very wicked
9 very strange
10 strange, odd, peculiar

Exercise 3 Adventure and romance

A
1 prison
2 a man who fought battles on horse back
3 a bow
4 travellers
5 spear
6 blade; sharp
7 public meal
8 arrows
9 towers; walls
10 long, sharp; knife
11 a prisoner's freedom
12 special
13 silk; cotton; cloth
14 covering; battle
15 fight; two; weapons

B
1 wonderful
2 red colour
3 very bright; shining
4 splendid
5 sparkle
6 guilty
7 good; grand
8 broken
9 looking
10 moment; bright